# TWO MEN CONTEMPLATING THE NATURE OF WOMEN AND THE UNIVERSE

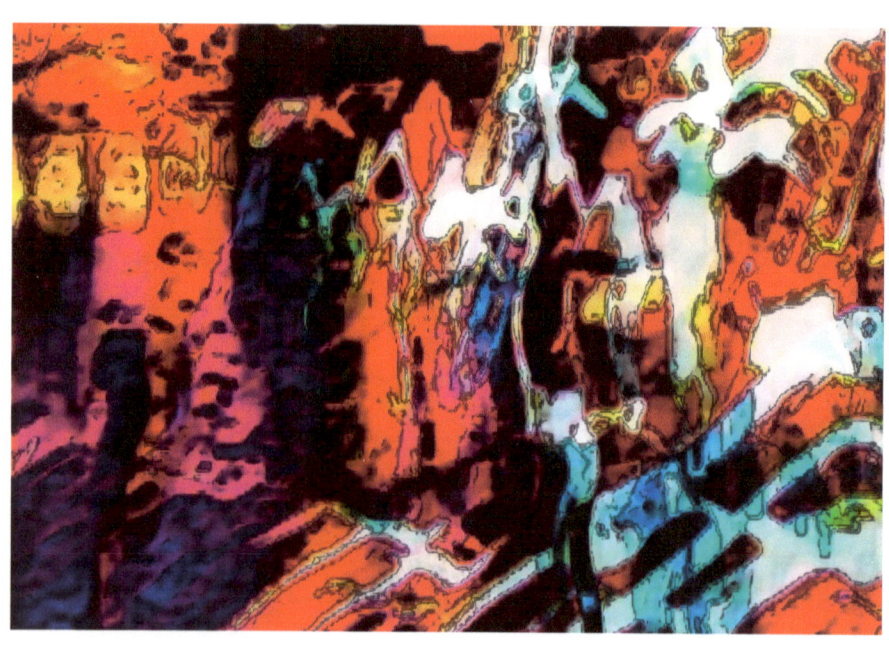

# TWO MEN CONTEMPLATING THE NATURE OF WOMEN AND THE UNIVERSE

## PRINT OPERAS

By

**Misha Ha Baka**

TWO MEN CONTEMPLATING THE NATURE OF

WOMEN AND THE UNIVERSE: Print Operas

ISBN-13: 978-0-9987941-8-1
ISBN-10: 0-9987941-8-X

Published by Ha Baka Book

First edition paperback 2017

# DEDICATION

For The Holy Father

And

The Divinity

# PRINT OPERAS

Two Men Contemplating the Nature of Women and the Universe ...................... 1

Two Men Contemplating the Nature of Women and the Universe BW .............. 2

Gaia ................................................................................................................ 3

Gaia BW ........................................................................................................ 4

Nursery .......................................................................................................... 5

Nursery BW ................................................................................................... 6

Circa 20000 BC ............................................................................................. 7

Circa 20000 BC BW ...................................................................................... 8

Dinosaur ........................................................................................................ 9

Dinosaur BW ............................................................................................... 10

Catfish ......................................................................................................... 11

Catfish BW .................................................................................................. 12

Grasshopper ................................................................................................ 13

Grasshopper BW ......................................................................................... 14

Pastoral ....................................................................................................... 15

Pastoral BW ................................................................................................ 16

Chariot ......................................................................................................... 17

Chariot BW .................................................................................................. 18

Motorcycle ................................................................................................... 19

Motorcycle BW ............................................................................................ 20

The Reed Sea .............................................................................................. 21

The Reed Sea BW ...................................................................22

Prayer ...................................................................23

Prayer BW ...................................................................24

Tribunal ...................................................................25

Tribunal BW ...................................................................26

Ship-A-Shore ...................................................................27

Ship-A-Shore BW ...................................................................28

Circus ...................................................................29

Circus BW ...................................................................30

Boulevard ...................................................................31

Boulevard BW ...................................................................32

Aperitif ...................................................................33

Aperitif BW ...................................................................34

Bouquet ...................................................................35

Bouquet BW ...................................................................36

Print Operas ...................................................................38

Additional Books by Misha Ha Baka ...................................................................39

MiKeigh Music ...................................................................40

As Tiny Tyke, the saga begins ...................................................................41

About the Artist & Author ...................................................................43

Before I began working on my current art project, I wanted to confirm the particular path I had chosen at this point in my life was the right one for me. I had been spending many, many hours using digital image manipulation software on the computer. This was a departure from the usual tools I had previously used to create my art with. Up until then, traditional medias such as inks, pastels, and paints of various types were my chosen tool. As I have previously done from time to time, I asked for confirmation that I was on the right road. I mentally asked for a clear, unmistakable "sign" that I was moving in the right direction. God can hear your thoughts very clearly. I didn't dwell on it and went about my usual way. In other words, I put it out there and continued about my business.

There have been other times that signs have occurred. Several times as a matter of fact, I could be walking on a road, and a hawk's feather comes fluttering down landing right by my foot. As I've gotten older, I've found the time between asking for the sign and it actually occurring has decreased. This time I didn't have to wait long for the response either, although it did catch me totally off guard and much by surprise.

It was now Sunday and as most Sundays go, I called the garage to bring my *toy car* up so I could take it for a spin downtown. That is where I usually went for brunch on the weekends. I had a favorite restaurant and usually parked the car in the same place at the same time each Sunday. One might call it a ritual of sorts. This time my car was the only one on that block. *Strange* I thought. I looked around to see if there were any "no parking police signs" or "parade notices" posted. There were none to be found, anywhere.

*Coincidence* I thought. I found an empty table that just happened to be facing towards the street where my car was parked. I ordered and was waiting on the slow service I was receiving when I notice a large truck with a huge beam on top of it pull along side of my car. The food finally came, it must have been two months after I had ordered it, but I finally started to eat. I was quite hungry.

I happened to glance out again and this time another large truck exactly the same as the first one pulled up in front of my car and secured itself in place. By now the first one had also secured itself in place. My car was blocked in, front and back. Saying I was a tad bit nervous was a considerable understatement. I sprinted out of the restaurant and went over to what looked like the leader of the group who was supervising the raising of several beams towards a huge, empty black cinder block wall on the side of a building directly behind my car.

"Sir, this is my car? Do I need to move it?"

"Don't worry. We aren't going to be here long, but if you want to move your car then we can easily move the trucks and let you get out."

I stood there with my jaw dropped, and mouth wide open.

He continued: "Rest assured that even with the heavy telescoping beams protruding out over your car, your car is very safe."

*Sure.* I said to myself, *Hey, it was insured. There was even gap insurance on it. If something happened, maybe I could get a car that didn't stink?*

He said they were putting up a sign on the side of the building. I had no clue as to what kind of sign they were putting up and didn't even ask. I went back to brunch since my food was getting cold. Of course, every second was now focused on the coming moment when the rolled up sign would drop. I got so distracted by the waitress who had brought me my check that I didn't even witness the unveiling of the sign. Sometimes it appears as if something conspires against things going as you planned, allowing some significant events to unravel themselves when you aren't looking.

When I had finished paying the check, I looked up and there was a huge canvas, several billboards high in size, suspended over the entire side of the building. This canvas billboard was advertising the specific branded software that I was using for the series of digital paintings I was now creating.

It wasn't until several hours later that I realized the full implications of what had just occurred. Yes, sometimes, the cool coupe kid is slow, slow, slow. I had just received a clear, unmistakable *sign* that I was moving in the right direction. I was pleased. I had gotten my confirmation. I continued with the creation of the current series, which I was working on. All though I didn't know it at the time, the completed digital paintings are ones that I used to later illustrate future books and music albums.

*Excerpted from Confessions of a Lonely Mystic short talk by Misha Ha Baka*

# TWO MEN CONTEMPLATING THE NATURE OF WOMEN AND THE UNIVERSE

The first two volumes of the Print Opera series of digital paintings are *Two Women Contemplating the Nature of the Universe: Print Operas BW* (in black and white) *and Two Women Contemplating the Nature of the Universe: Print Operas (in color)*. Volumes 3 and 4 of the Print Opera series of digital paintings are *Two Women, Three Flamingoes and a Pooch: Print Operas (in color) and Two Women, Three Flamingoes and a Pooch: Print Operas BW (in black and white)*. This new work is the 5th installment of the Print Opera series and contains both the color and black and white versions of the digital prints. These artworks are signed and meticulously self-published on fine art paper using gicleé with inks and papers rated high for permanency and are faithfully reproduced in this book. They are also for sale as unsigned reproductions.

Abstract art is just that – abstract. However, for me, it is *fun* to see the *stract* in the *abstract*. While I was creating the series, my two women from Volume 1 made an encore performance in a second painting. Looking at the original painting of *Two Women Contemplating the Nature of the Universe*, I was surprised to see two female looking figures in the lower left-hand corner looking up at the rest of the painting. In Volume 3 they reappeared in the lower right-hand corner of the painting and brought along three flamingoes and their pooch. They must enjoy going for leisurely strolls. I was very much surprised when the women reappeared a second time, but I was even more surprised when two males appeared in the lower left-hand corner of a third painting. This added to the fact that there were faint glimmers of two women in the lower right-hand corner as well as one of the original ones with hands crossed, looking down at the two men. The men were looking right up at her, but I'm not sure that they noticed her. It looked like she noticed them. So the question now became: What were these two men looking at and what were they thinking?

Of course, they could be contemplating the nature of the universe as were the ladies, but then again, they could be contemplating the nature of the ladies; a subject which often commands the attention of men. Since the women were showing up again and since they don't like to be excluded from a party, I included them in the men's book. As the ladies were already dressed in white, I displayed their comments alongside black and white versions of the color paintings so that I didn't get confused about who was doing the speaking. As the men may have noticed them wandering around, I asked them about this and they responded by saying that they wanted to comment on the series of new paintings, but their first remarks were to be on the women...

Thank you for visiting my literary art gallery yet again. For the first time visitor, you are invited to visit the other Print Operas. *Enjoy your visit...*

Misha Ha Baka  2017

# TWO MEN CONTEMPLATING THE NATURE OF WOMEN AND THE UNIVERSE

# Two Men Contemplating the Nature of Women and the Universe

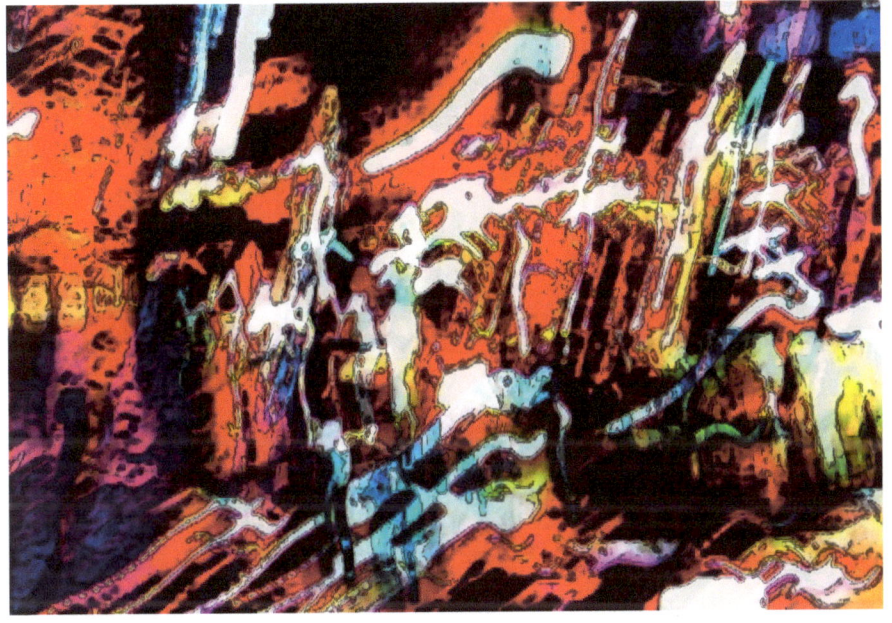

"Did they really think that they were going to have the last word?"
"Never mind that; how do we rearrange what they moved to the left?"


"Why do I have a feeling they are talking behind our backs?"
"They could be in front of us, and we wouldn't understand what they said."

# Two Men Contemplating the Nature of Women and the Universe BW

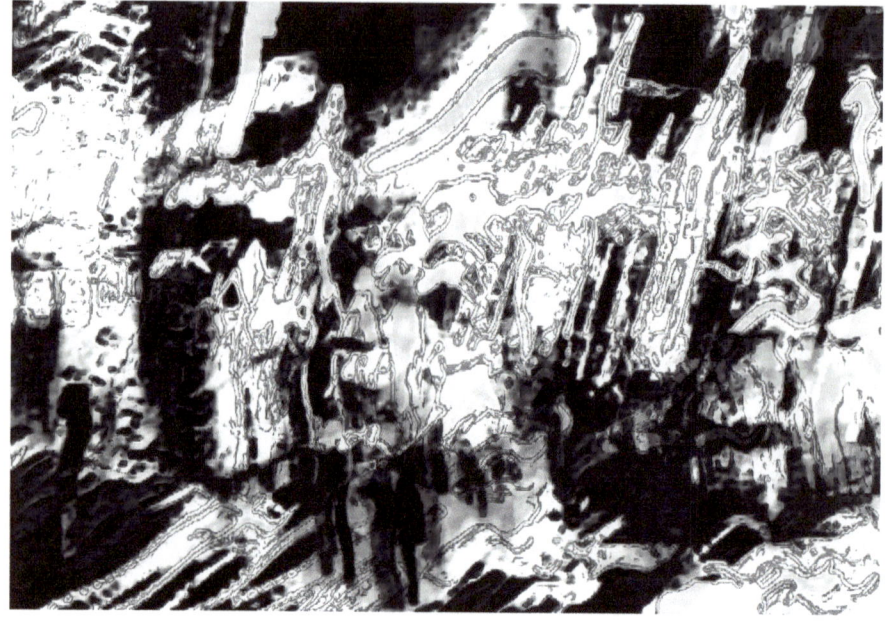

"They have a lot of nerve using our format for their advantage."
"Par for the course, we have always been the trailblazers, Honey!"


"Do you think they can hear us?"
"They can hear everything; they just don't want to listen."


"Who invited the Flamingoes, and why is there a snake hovering above?"
"I wouldn't worry about it, they already ate the apple."

# GAIA

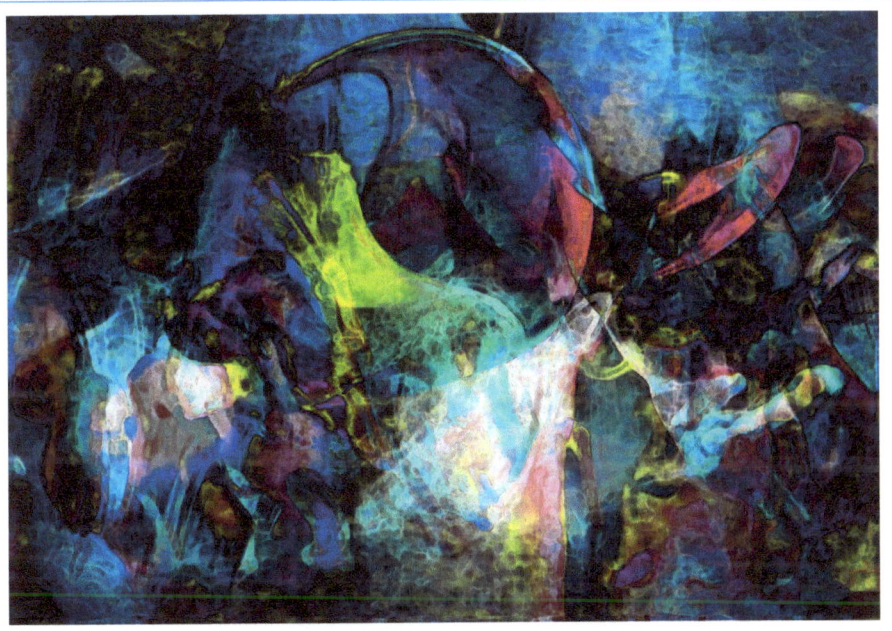

"She has done a great job with the planet."
"I'm hoping we don't have to set things right again like last time."

# GAIA BW

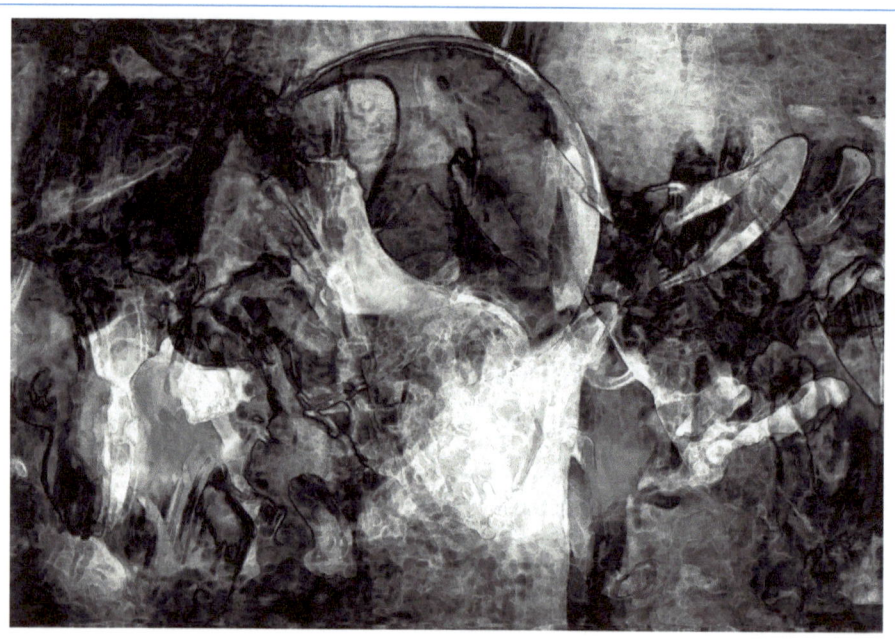

"Did we actually hear a compliment from their lips?"
"I heard it too, they must be inhaling."

# Nursery

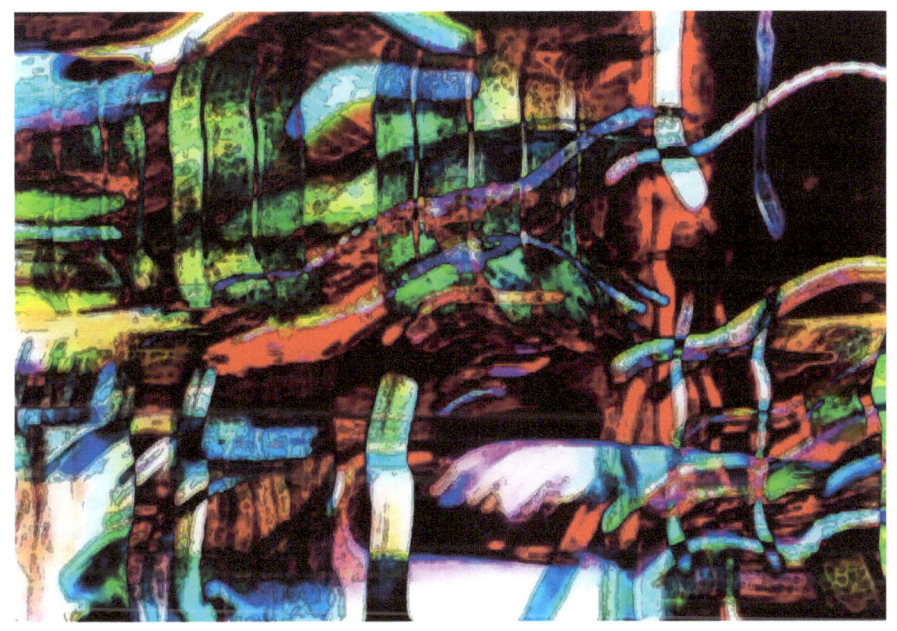

"As much as they complain, they must realize that we had a small part to play in their creation."

"Yes, I'm sure that they will emphasize the *small* part."

# NURSERY BW

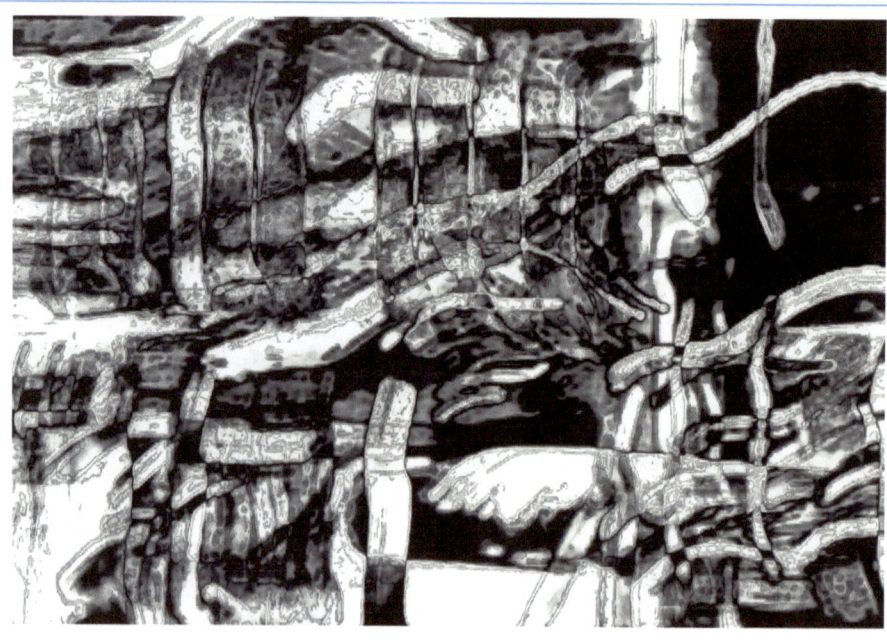

"How come they get half the credit?"
"I know, for them, it's a quick poof and we deal with it for months..."

# CIRCA 20000 BC

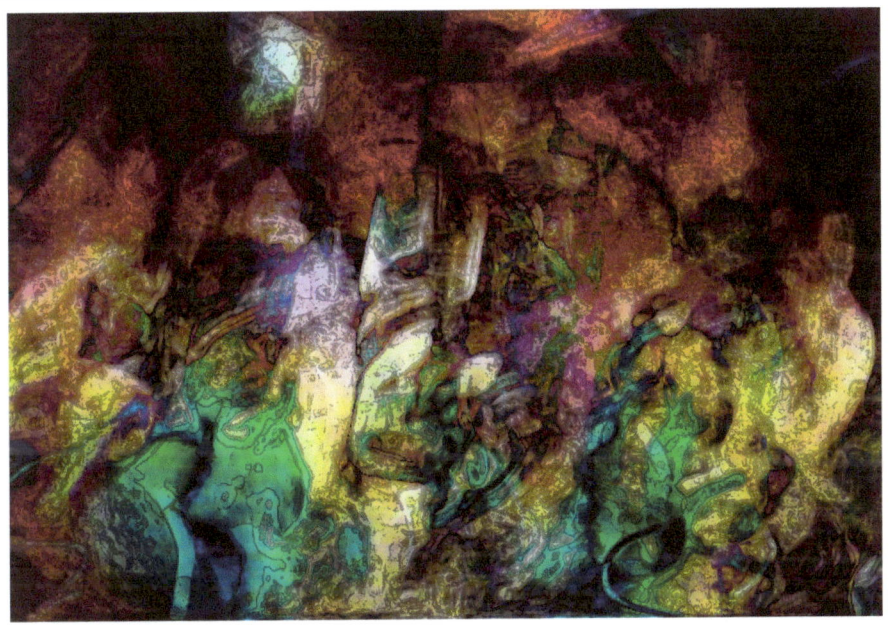

"Life was so simple then, no smartphones."
"Life is simple now too, only we've become too complicated."

# CIRCA 20000 BC BW

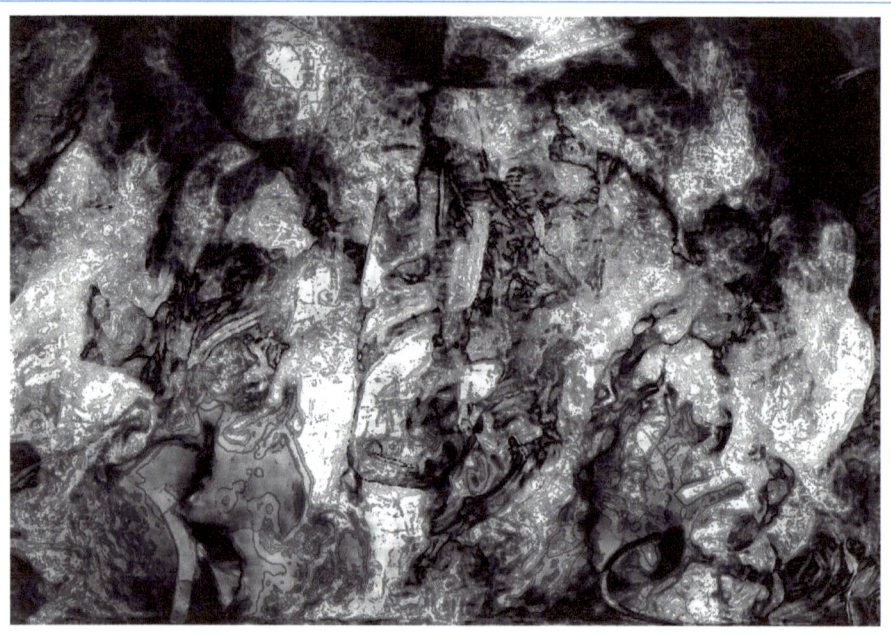

"I don't think we are complicated."
"True: Love, babies a good career, a strong 401K, nice car, jewelry..."

# DINOSAUR

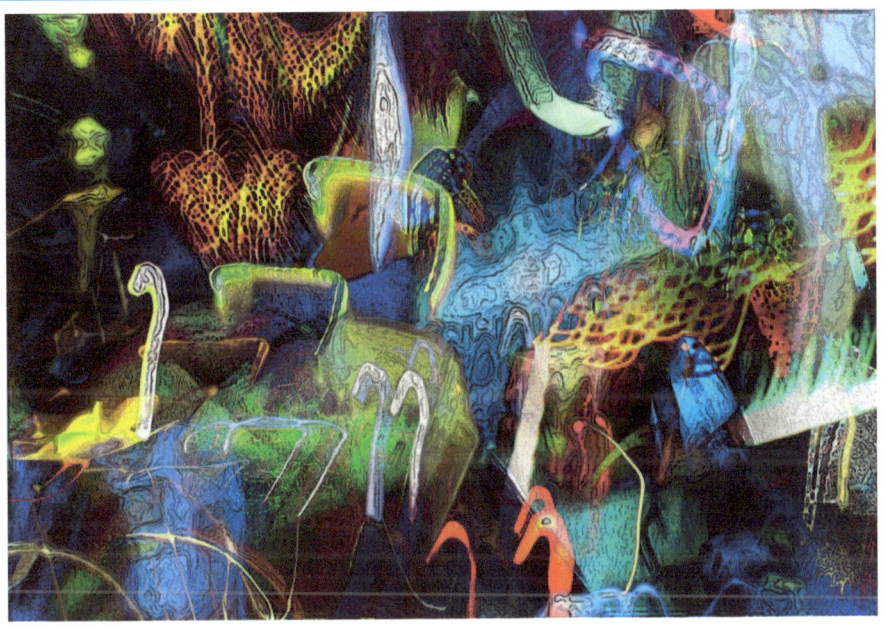

"I was sorry to see them have to leave."
"Me too, not everything lasts forever."

# DINOSAUR BW

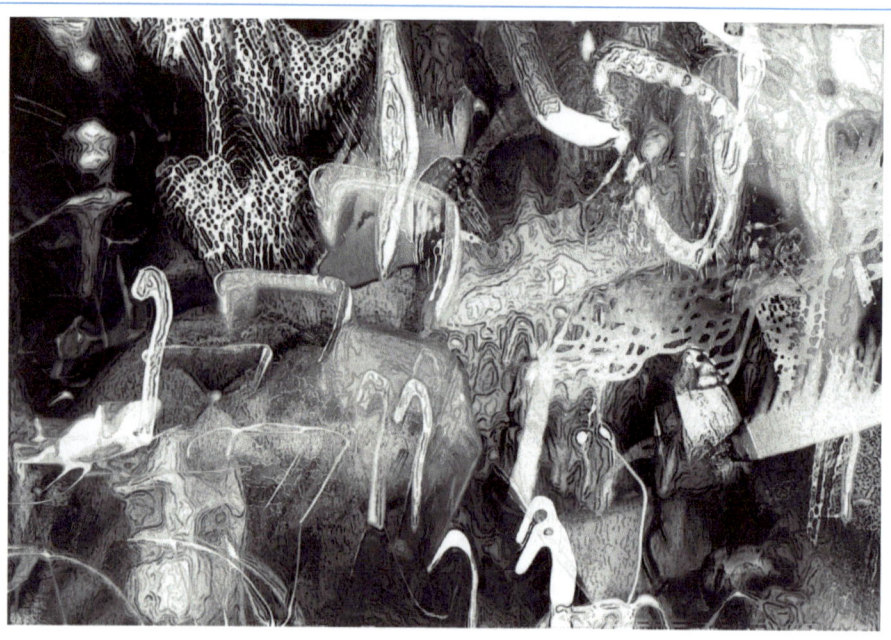

"I told him that Rex needs to go for a walk."
"Like everything else, they do it on their time, which is now gone."

# CATFISH

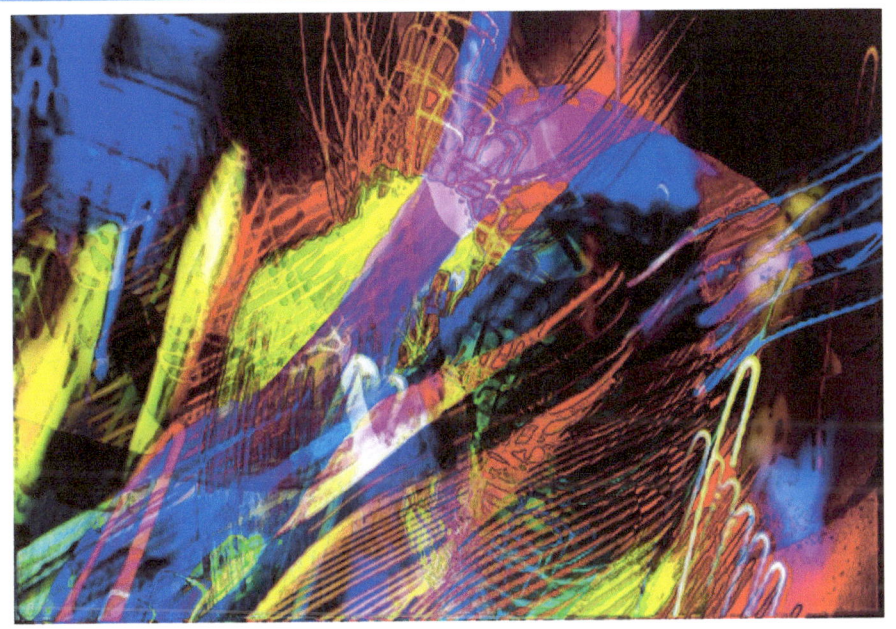

"What came first, the cat or the fish?"
"Good Question. Why not ask them?
They seem to have an answer for everything, even if it hasn't been asked."

# CATFISH BW

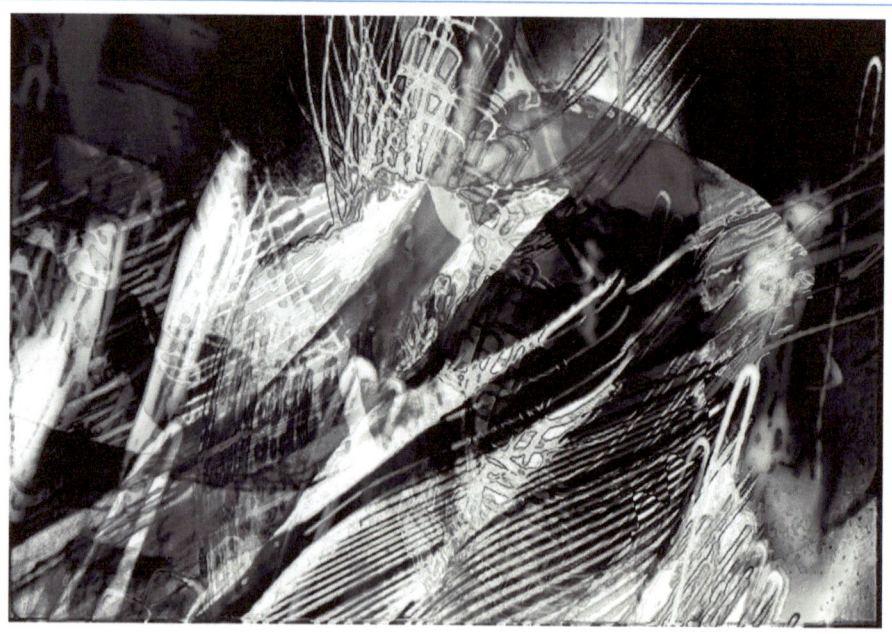

"Sometimes I think they are fishing for compliments."
"Let 'em wait. They can't keep the cat in the bag for too long."

# GRASSHOPPER

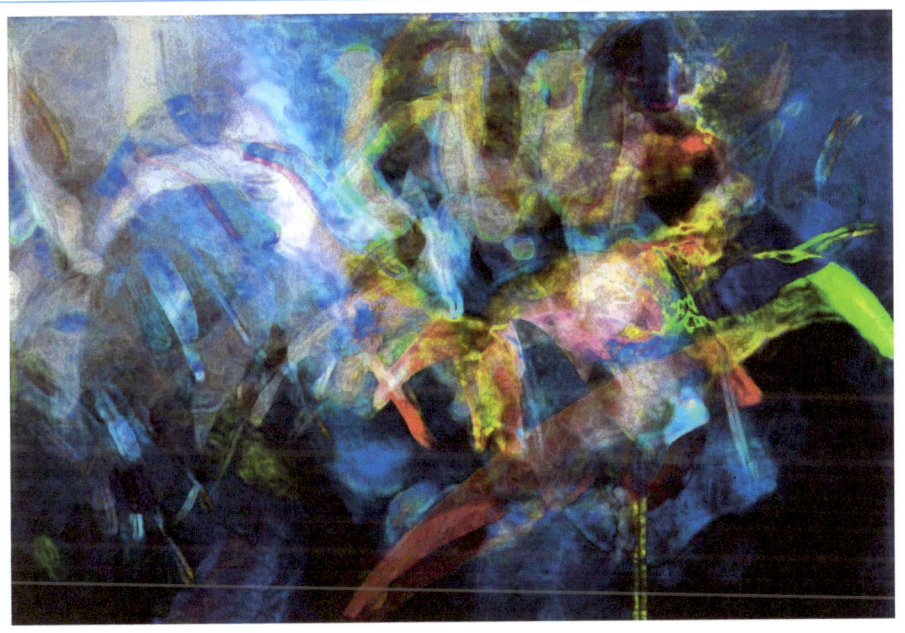

"Sometimes I feel like I'm all over the place."
"Maybe it's because you actually are everywhere?"

# GRASSHOPPER BW

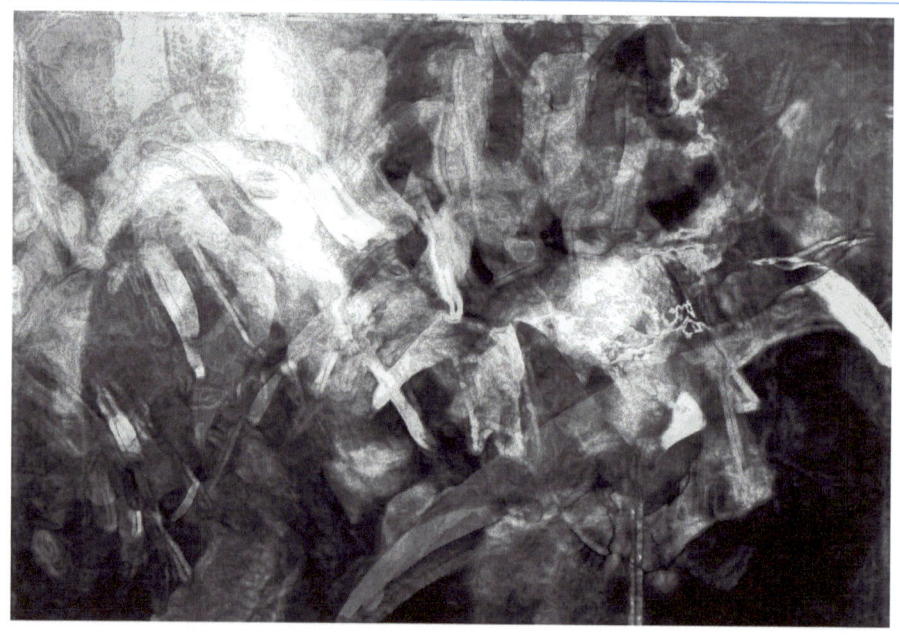

"Do you ever think they will ever let us forget that without them we'd be without us?"
"Are you kidding? You know they never forget anything about us, but when it comes to them – selective memory!"

# PASTORAL

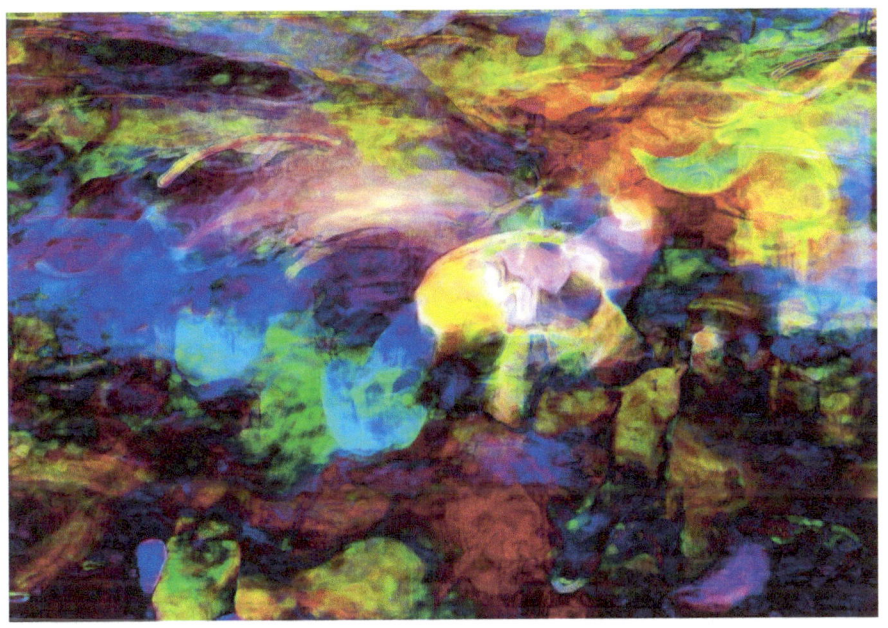

"When it comes to gardening, how come they get the flowers and we dig the dirt?"

"You've got it wrong. Don't you go and get the flowers for them too?"

# PASTORAL BW

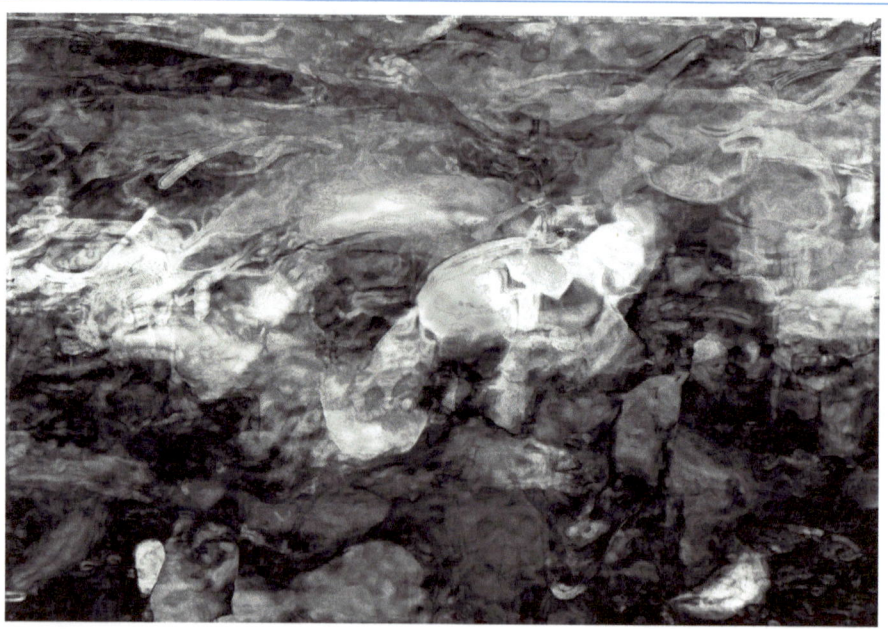

"In spite of all the aggregation, a good bouquet can turn the tables."
"I've had them turn the tables on me without a good or bad bouquet."

# CHARIOT

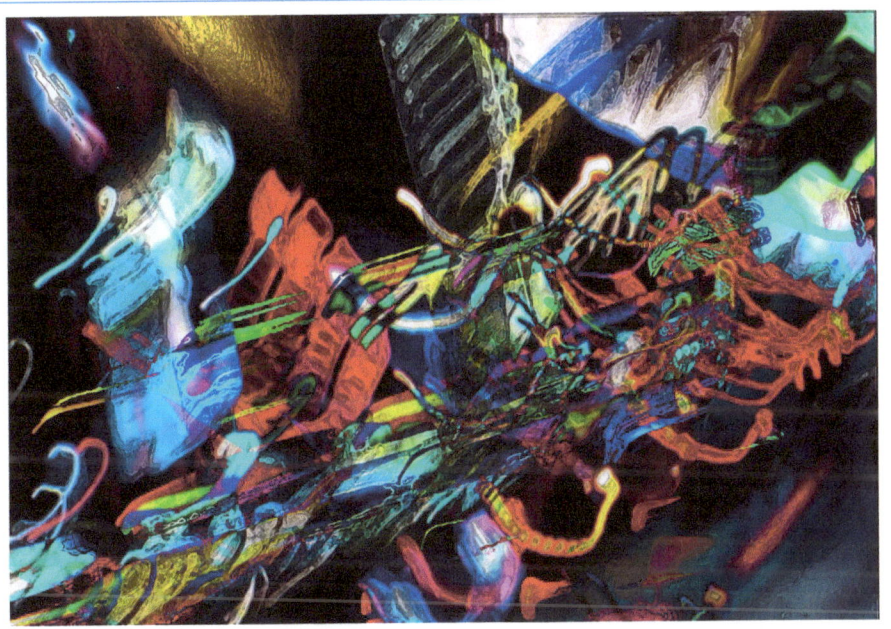

"Remember how it felt to steer those steeds around?"
"We made those horses proud."

## CHARIOT BW

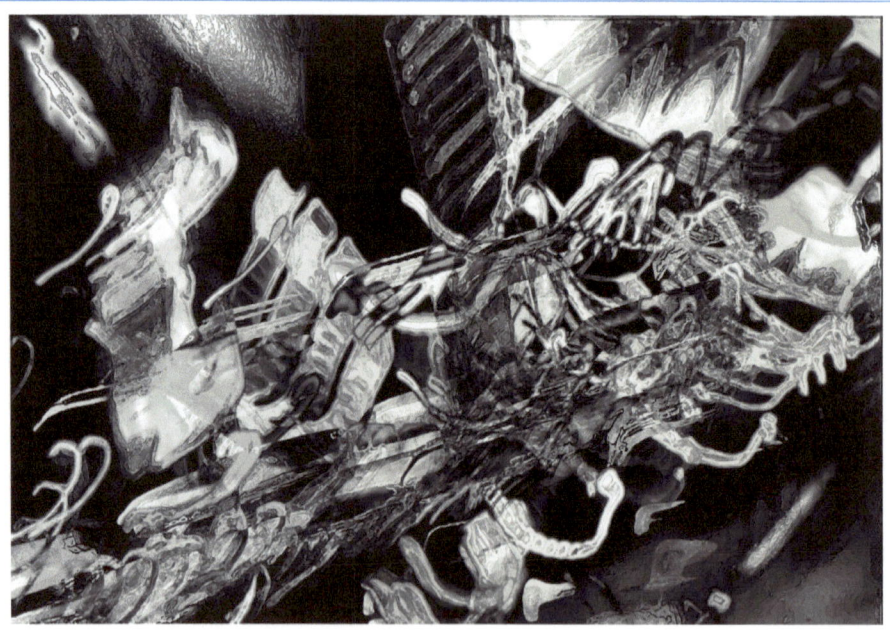

"They still need to feel like they have the reins."
"I know – they still measure their thrust in horsepower."

# MOTORCYCLE

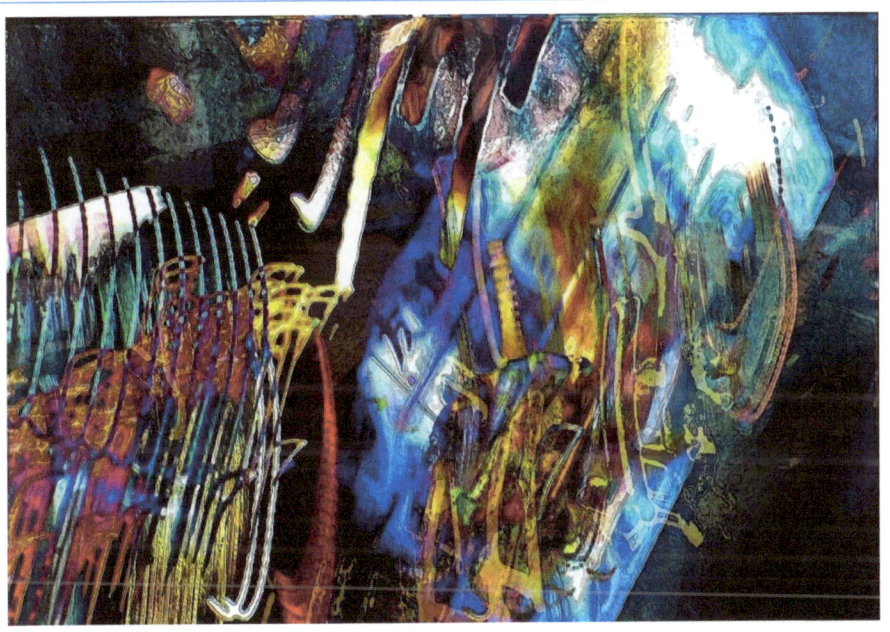

"My new *chariot* pops quite a wallop!"
"Yes and *Varoooom* sounds so much better then *Giddy-Up*."

# MOTORCYCLE BW

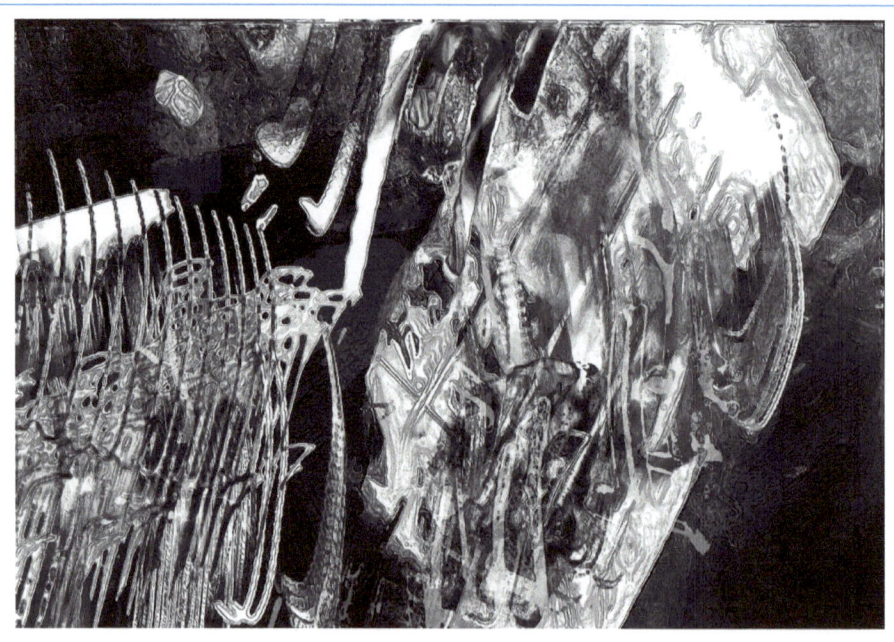

"I am happy that we can drive those beasts too."
"Can you imagine, initially we only sat in that little sidecar."

# THE REED SEA

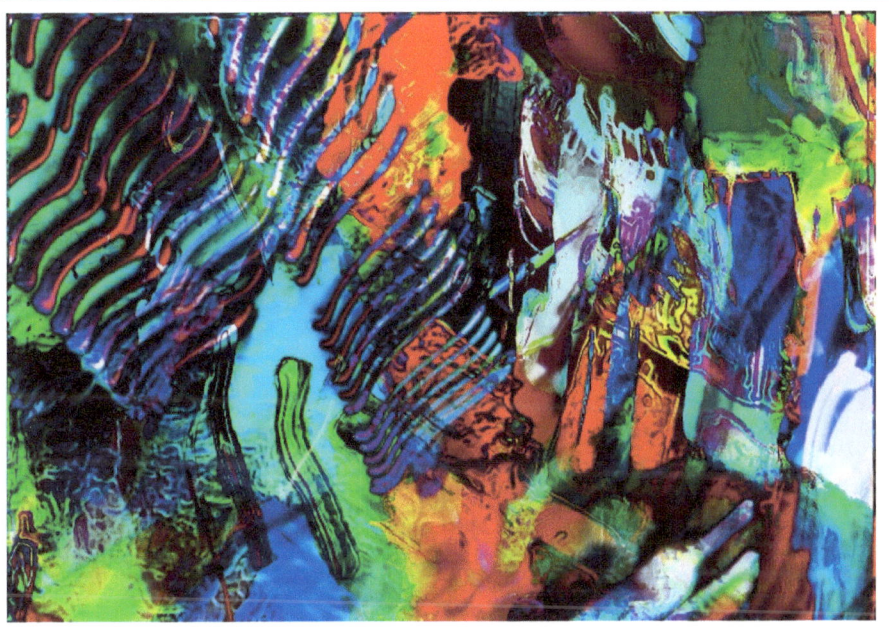

"I must admit, I like showing off occasionally."
"Memories like those last forever."

# THE REED SEA BW

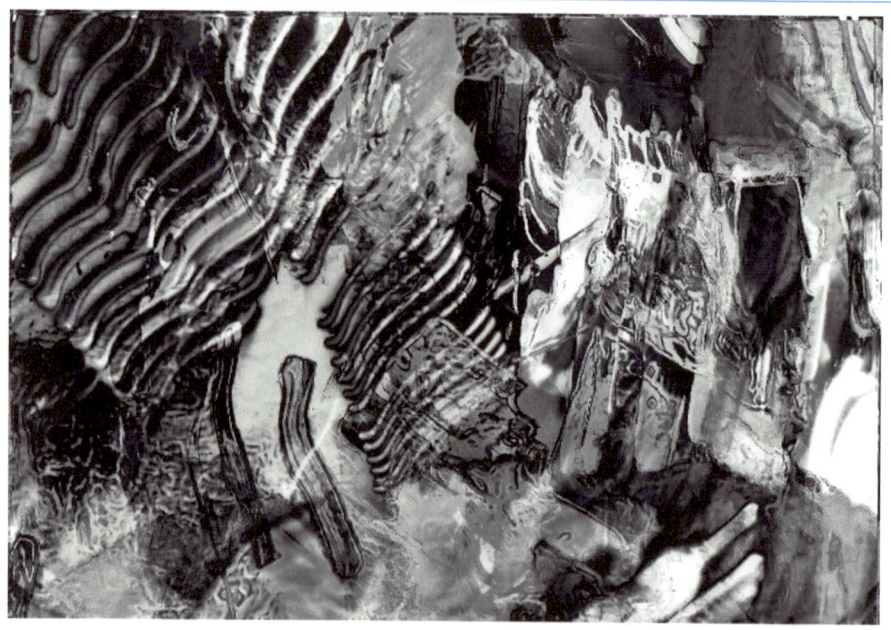

"I don't get it. They make miracles and we dance with timbrels?"
"Not too bad, where would the movie be without the soundtrack?"

# PRAYER

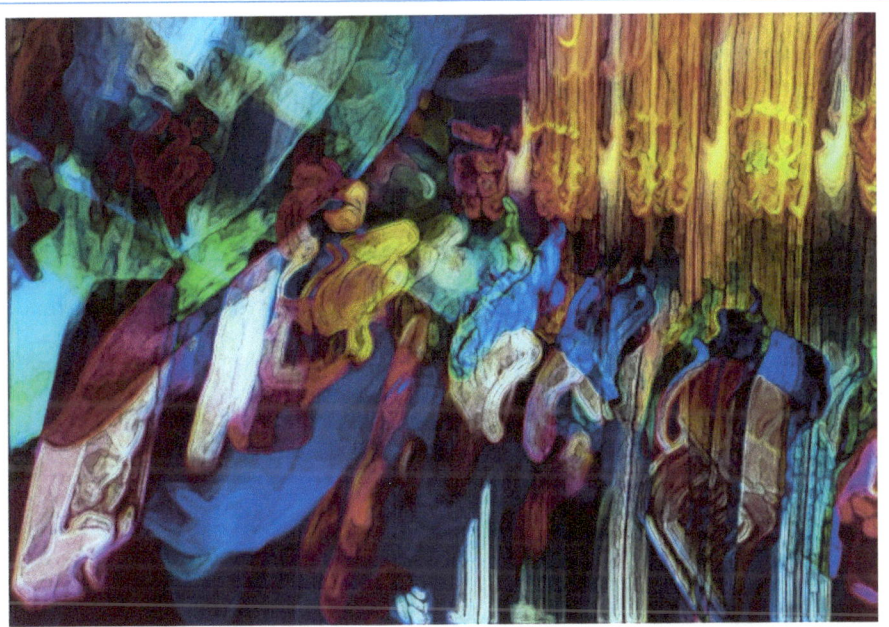

"Do you think they realize we hear every single thought?"
"No, they think we hear it only if they specifically ask us to listen."

# PRAYER BW

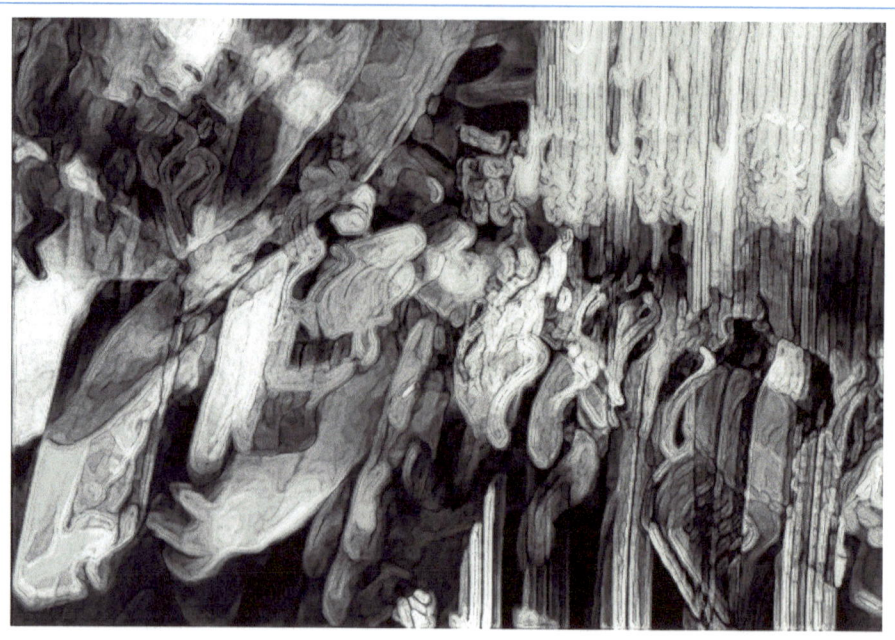

"I get lots of requests also."
"It's a good thing that we can do a thing or two too."

# TRIBUNAL

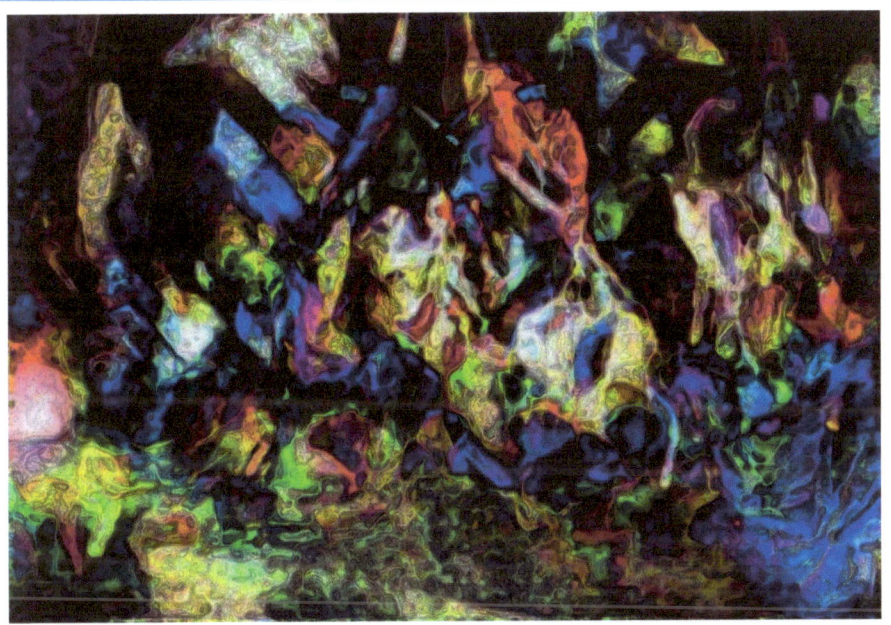

"Sitting around the campfire and sharing life stories is true bonding."
"Yes, and hopefully there will still be trees to feed the fires."

# TRIBUNAL BW

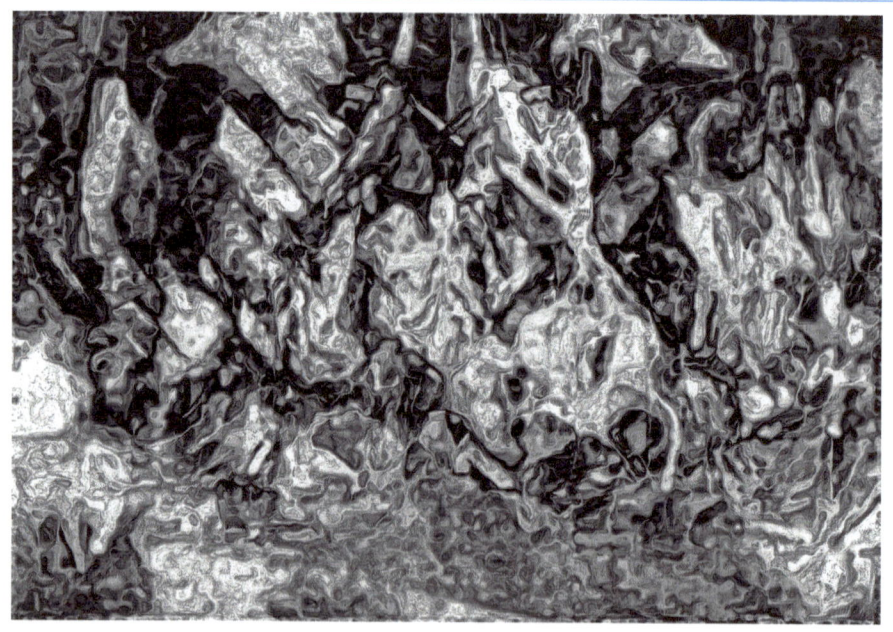

"Do you think we will ever make it to the top?"
"We already are on top, they only think we aren't."

# SHIP-A-SHORE

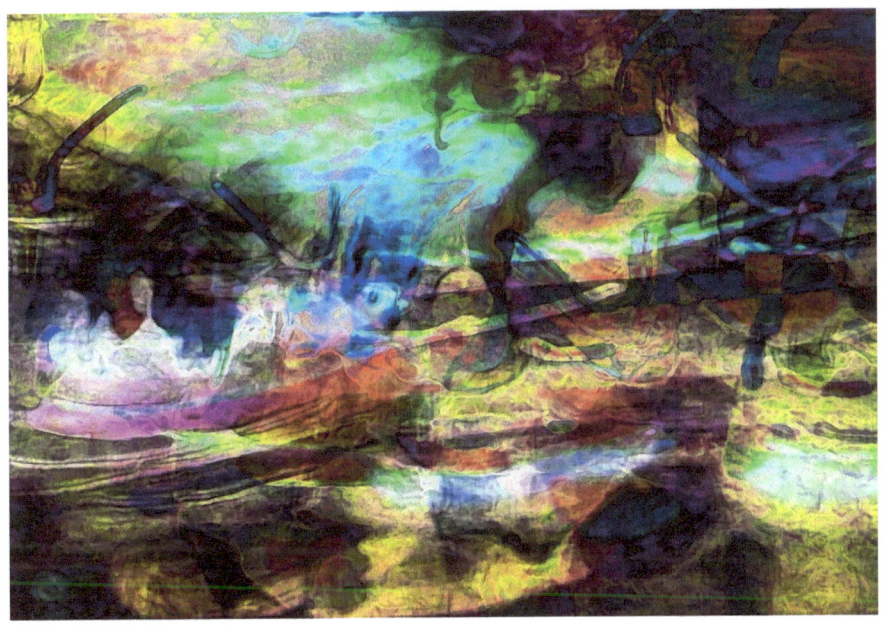

"Our ships are still sailing out with billions more set to sail."
"Yes, that bang is still banging away."

## Ship-A-Shore BW

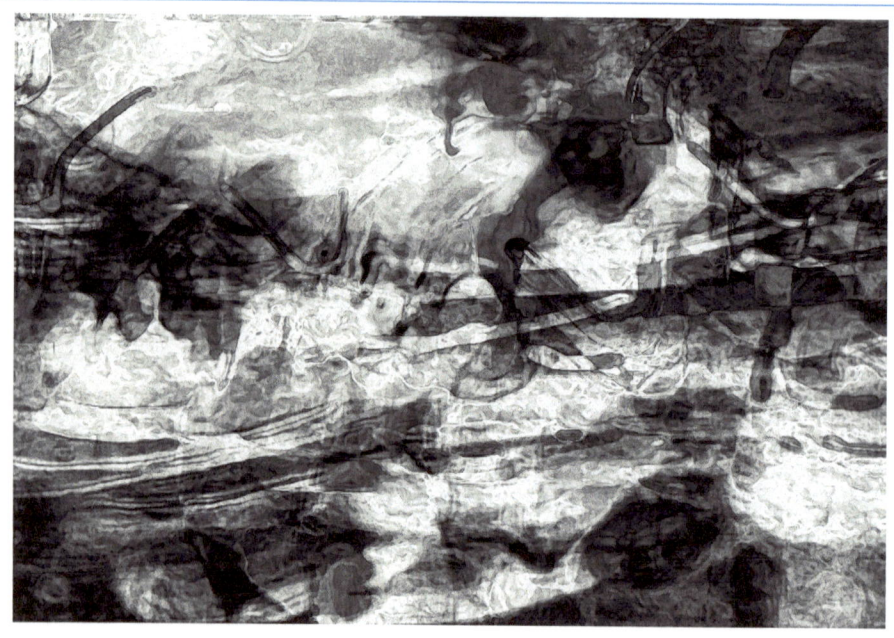

"Big deal, so they have a huge fleet and a big bang."
"Of course they forget they are sailing on *our* waters."

# Circus

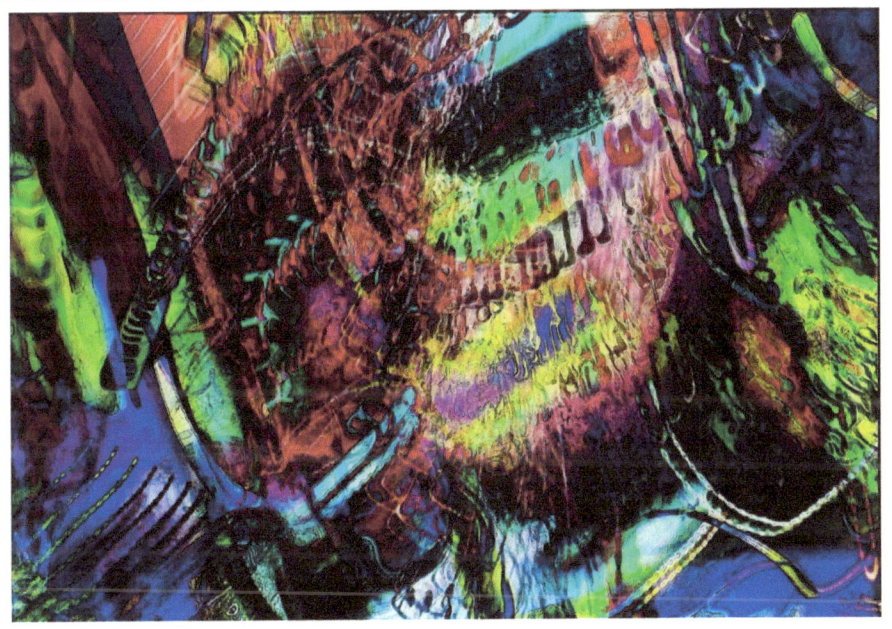

"I know sometimes it looks like a three ring circus down there."
"If everything was perfect from the start, what would the caregivers do?"

# CIRCUS BW

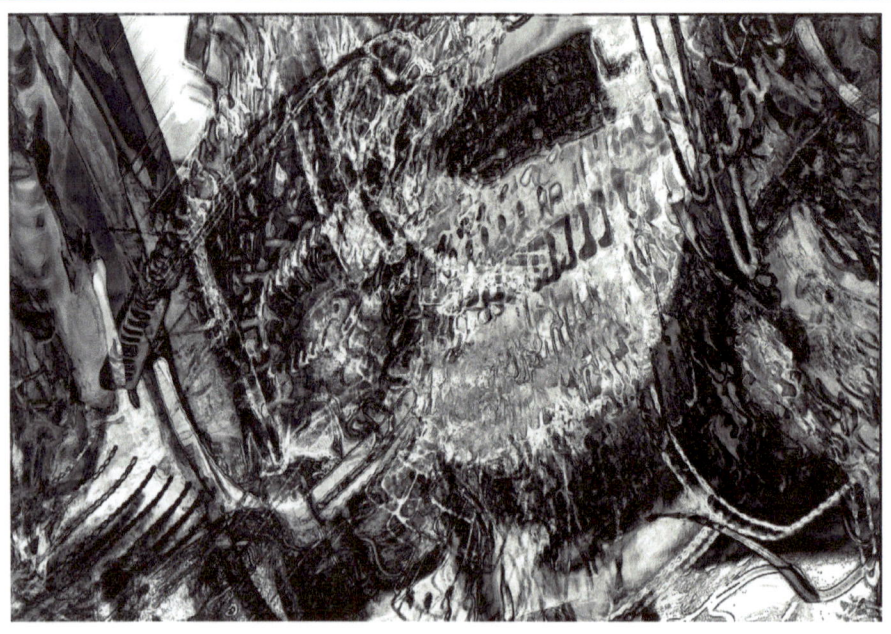

"I thought of joining the circus when I was younger."
"Circus? Doesn't life already turn you upside down and right side up?"

# BOULEVARD

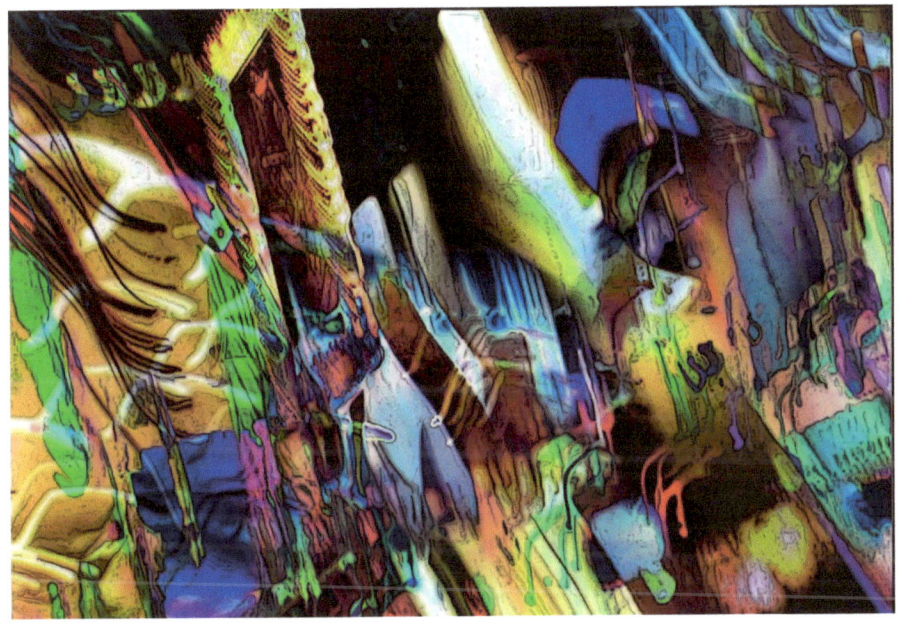

"I enjoy the occasional leisurely stroll along the avenue."
"Your five-minute walk to the store is not a leisurely stroll."

## BOULEVARD BW

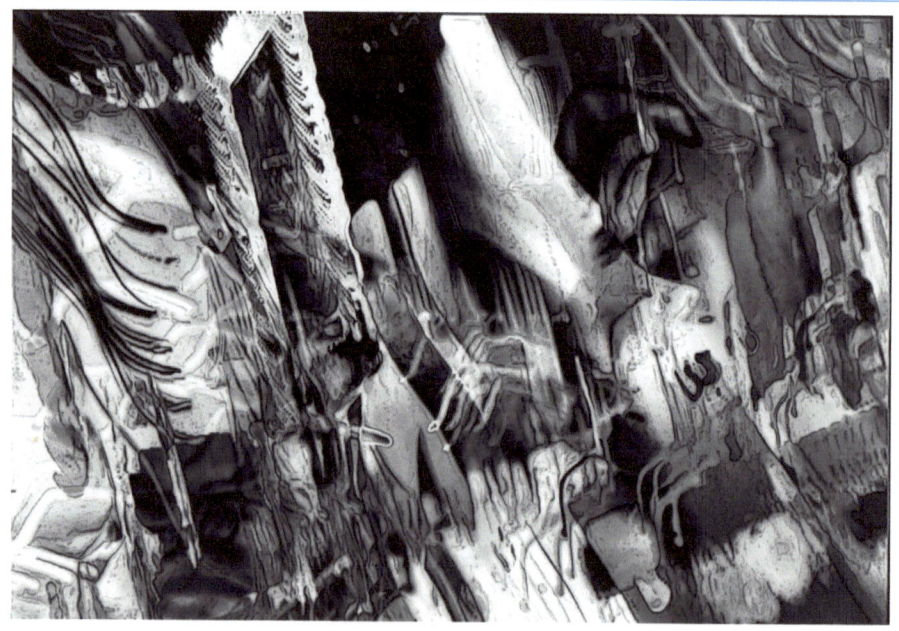

"Doesn't he realize you can't buy everything in only five minutes?"
"No, because that's how long everything they do lasts."

# APERITIF

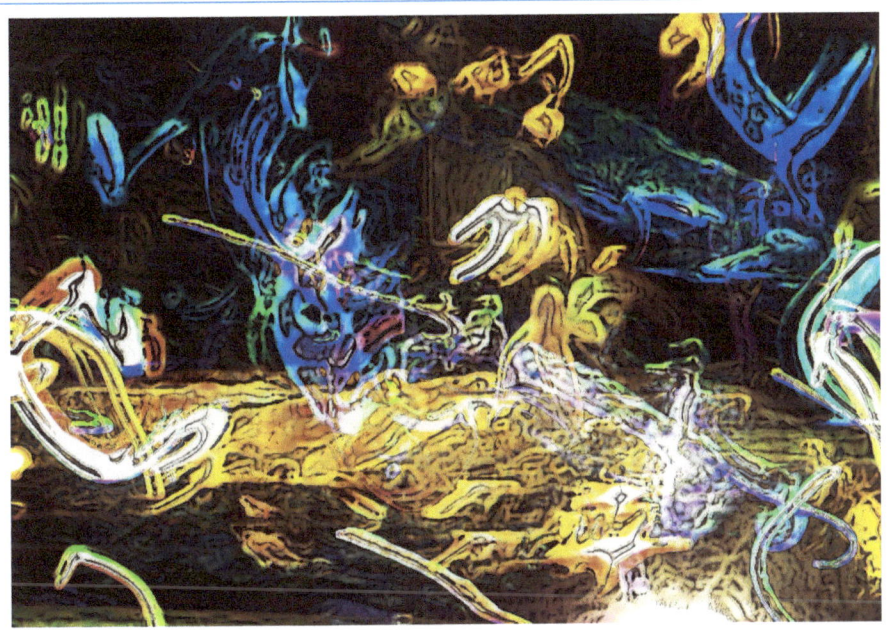

"Luckily they figured out how to make booze."
"*They*? Why do you think they call it *spirits*?"

# Aperitif BW

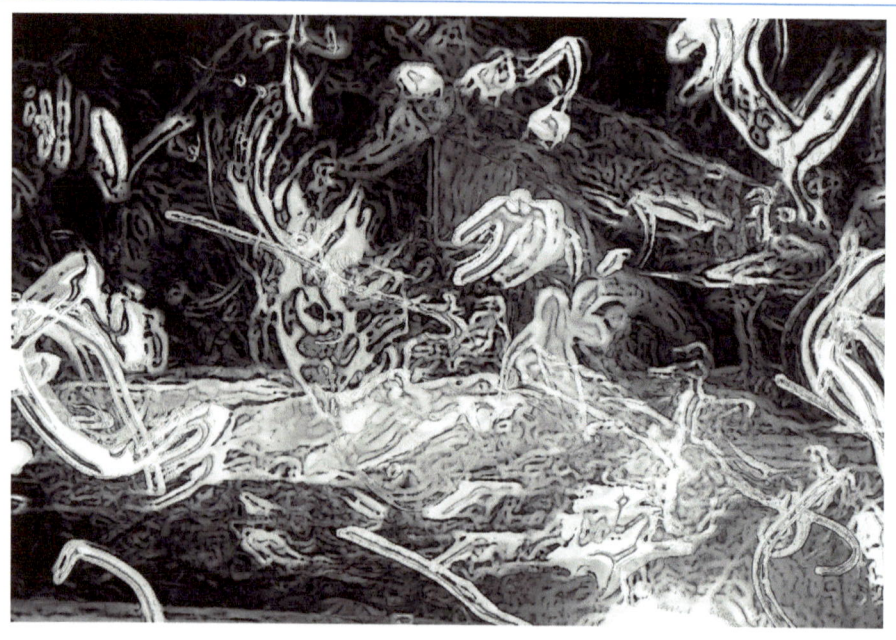

"I enjoy a stiff drink every once and a while."
"Stiff is good even if it's only once in a while."

# BOUQUET

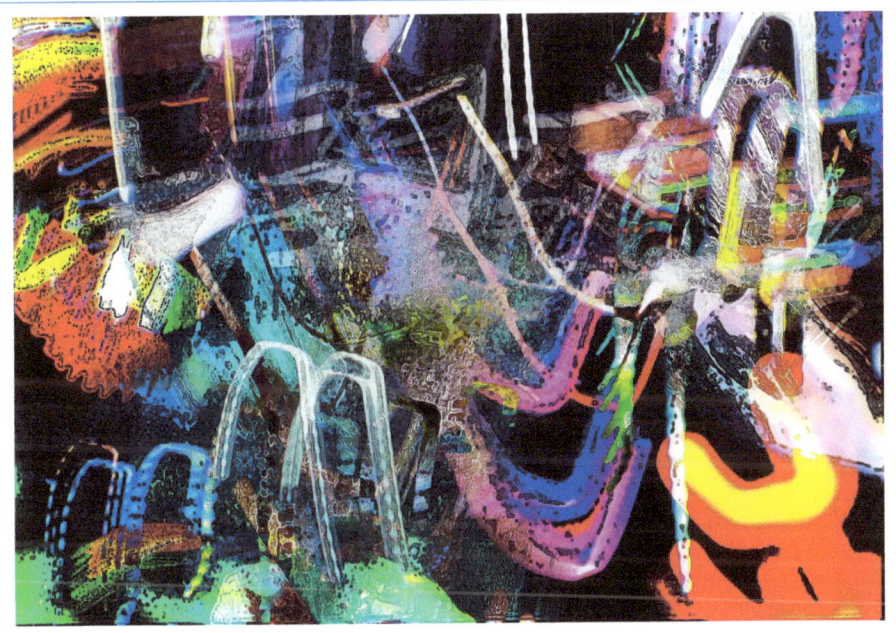

"When all else fails, we can always give flowers..."
"Yes and if that fails there are those colorless, glass-like sparkling stones."

# Bouquet BW

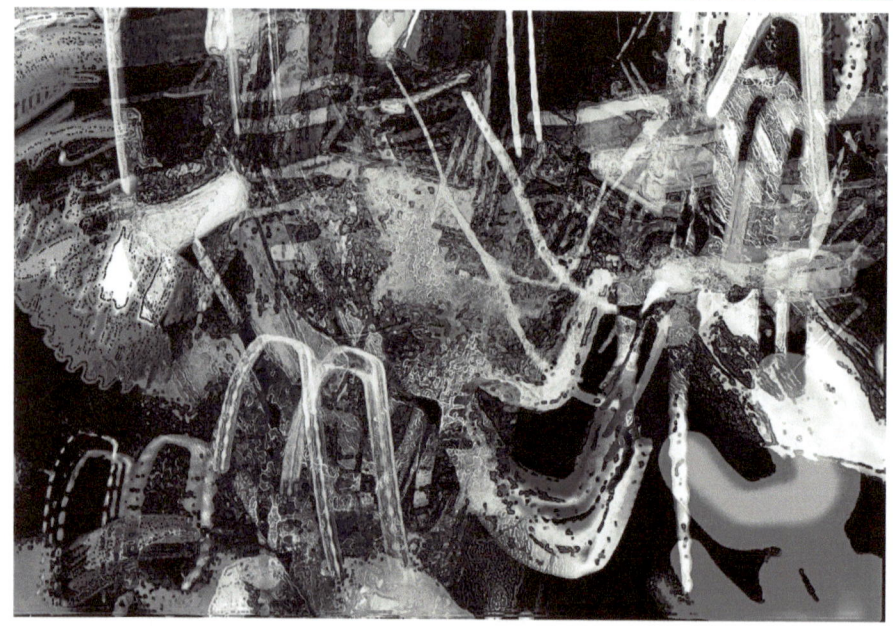

"Flowers, chocolates and baubles don't cut it anymore."
"I know. We need the right stuff: Love, love, love…"

# PRINT OPERAS

Aperitif, 33

Aperitif BW, 34

Boulevard, 31

Boulevard BW, 32

Bouquet, 35

Bouquet BW, 36

Catfish, 11

Catfish BW, 12

Chariot, 17

Chariot BW, 18

Circa 20000 BC, 7

Circa 20000 BC BW, 8

Circus, 29

Circus BW, 30

Dinosaur, 9

Dinosaur BW, 10

Gaia, 3

Gaia BW, 4

Grasshopper, 13

Grasshopper BW, 14

Motorcycle, 19

Motorcycle BW, 20

Nursery, 5

Nursery BW, 6

Pastoral, 15

Pastoral BW, 16

Prayer, 23

Prayer BW, 24

Ship-A-Shore, 27

Ship-A-Shore BW, 28

The Reed Sea, 21

The Reed Sea BW, 22

Tribunal, 25

Tribunal BW, 26

Two Men Contemplating the Nature of
   Women and the Universe, 1

Two Men Contemplating the Nature of
   Women and the Universe BW, 2

## ADDITIONAL BOOKS BY MISHA HA BAKA

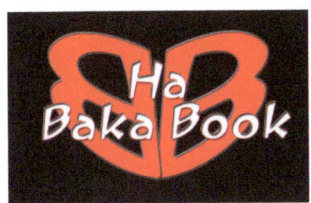

www.habakabook.com

Look for another volume of the *Print Opera* series coming very soon.

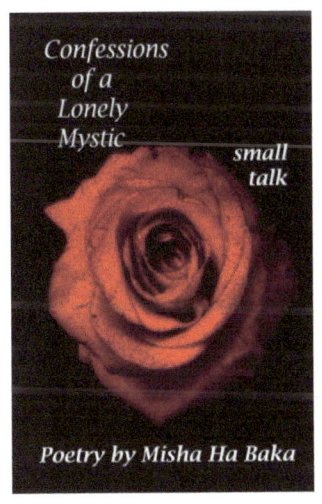

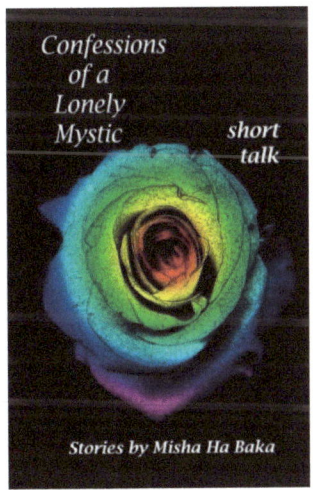

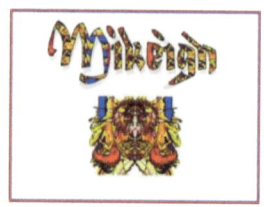

# MIKEIGH MUSIC

**Available for purchase at www.mikeigh.com.**

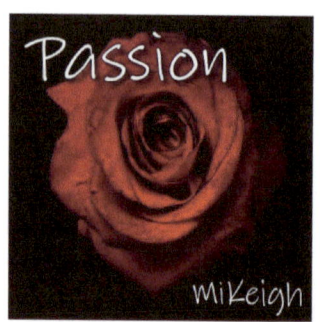

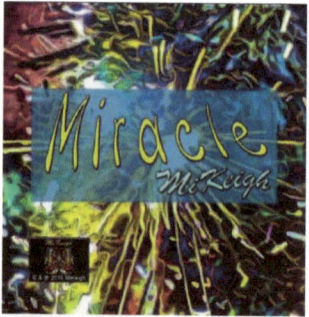

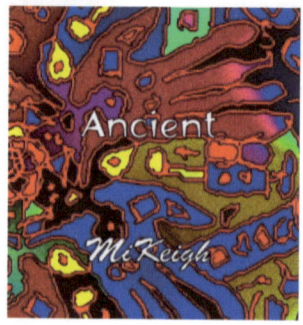

# *The Lonely Mystic*

## As Tiny Tyke, the saga begins

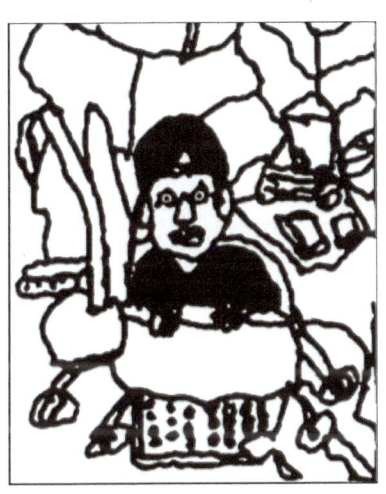

"I'm not in a stroller,

This is a High Roller!"

Excerpted from

*Portraits of a Lonely Mystic in 3D*

For my beloved wherever she may be...

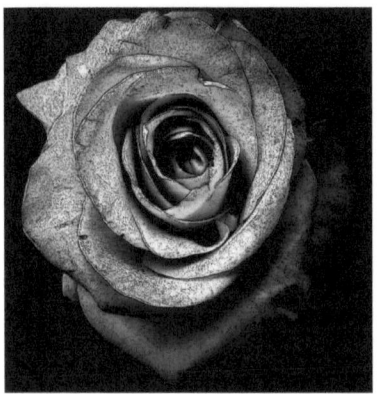

# ABOUT THE ARTIST & AUTHOR

Misha Ha Baka has worn many hats during his professional career. He holds a BA in English Literature, an MA in Asian Studies and has studied healing and mystic thought in Asia, England, Israel, and the United States. He is an ordained spiritual healer and ordained member of the clergy. He is a fine artist, a graphic artist, a photographer, a musician, and a composer with dozens of albums of original music including *Passion*, *Miracle*, and *Ancient*.

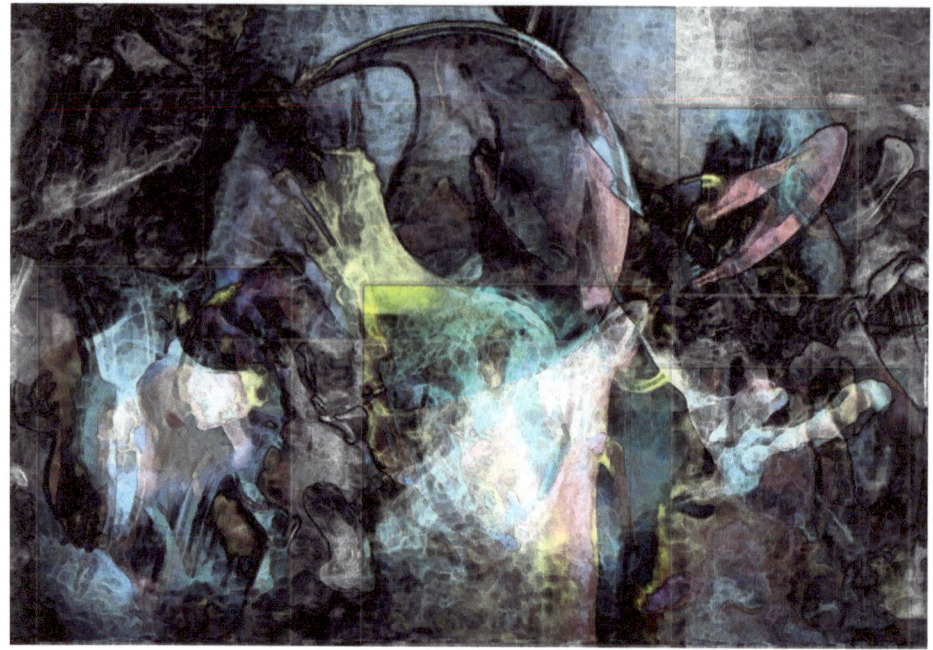

It appears that our men and women have not only been roaming around in the first painting, figures have now shown up in Gaia also. What are they doing and what is that red object?

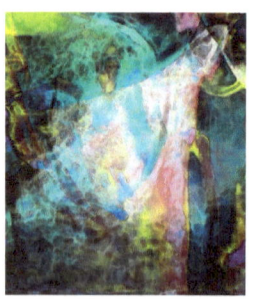 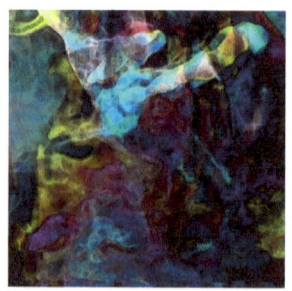 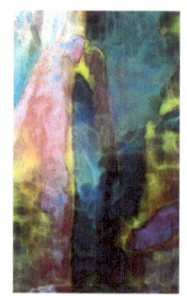

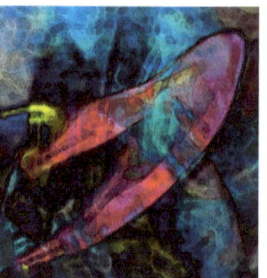

to be continued…